THE**NILE**

a journey along some of the
world's great rivers

This edition published 2010 by
Evans Brothers Limited
2a Portman Mansions
Chiltern Street
London W1U 6NR

Commissioned by: Su Swallow
Consultant: Stephen Watts; Peter A. Clayton
Design: Neil Sayer
Editors: Debbie Fox and Jayne Booth
Picture research: Victoria Brooker
Maps: Hardlines

British Library Cataloguing in Publication Data.

Pollard, Michael, 1931 -
 The Nile. - (Great rivers)
 1. Nile River - Juvenile literature 2.Nile River Valley -
 Juvenile literature
 I.Title
 962

 ISBN 9780237541163

Printed in Singapore

© Evans Brothers Limited 1997

ACKNOWLEDGEMENTS

For permission to reproduce copyright material, the author
and publishers gratefully acknowledge the following:

Cover: (background images) Fotolia (from top) Bergerot-Robert/Still Pictures, Jeremy Hartley/Panos Pictures, Stephanie Colasanti, Nigel Francis/Robert Harding Picture Library **page 8** David Keith Jones/Images of Africa **page 9** Earth Satellite Corporation/Science Photo Library **page 10** Ursula Reif/Images of Africa **page 11** (top) David Beatty/Robert Harding Picture Library (bottom) CNES, 1989 Distribution Spot image/Science Photo Library **page 12** Jeremy Horner/Tony Stone Images **page 13** (left) Peter Clayton (right) Stephanie Colasanti **page 14** Ecoscene/Sally Morgan **page 15** (top) Robert Harding Picture Library (bottom) Robert Harding Picture Library **page 16** Mary Evans Picture Library **page 17** (left) Trip/P Mitchell (right) Trip/D Saunders **page 18** Ecoscene/Simon Grove **page 19** Royal Geographical Society **page 20** T De Salis/Still Pictures **page 21** (top) Trygve Bølstad/Panos Pictures (bottom) Jim Holmes/Panos Pictures **page 22** Trip/P Joynson-Hicks **page 23** (left) David Keith Jones (right) David Keith Jones/Images of Africa **page 24** Bruce Coleman Ltd **page 25** Katri Burri/Panos Pictures **page 26** Mark Edwards/Still Pictures **page 27** Christine Osborne Pictures **page 28** Dominic Harcourt-Webster/Panos Pictures **page 29** (top right) Sassoon/Robert Harding Picture Library (bottom left) Trip/H Rogers **page 30** (left) Terence Spencer/Colorific (right) David Keith Jones/Images of Africa **page 31** Stephanie Colasanti **page 32** Ecoscene/Sally Morgan **page 33** (right) David Keith Jones/Images of Africa (left) Ecoscene/Sally Morgan **page 34** Nigel Francis/Robert Harding Picture Library **page 35** (top) Yves Debay/Image Bank (bottom) Earth Satellite Corporation/Science Photo Library **page 36** Jeremy Hartley/Panos Pictures **page 37** (top) Tony Stone Images (bottom) Christine Osborne Pictures **page 38** Peter Cadot/Images of Africa **page 39** (top) Bergerot-Robert/Still Pictures (bottom) Tom McHugh/Oxford Scientific Films **page 40** David Keith Jones/Images of Africa **page 41** (top) Robert Harding Picture Library (bottom) Ursula Reif/Images of Africa **page 42** (left) Katri Burri/Panos Pictures (right) Associated Press **page 43** (left) Israel Talby/Robert Harding (right) David Keith Jones/Images of Africa

CONTENTS

THE LONGEST RIVER

THE NILE IS THE LONGEST RIVER IN THE WORLD, FLOWING FOR NEARLY 6700 KILOMETRES FROM ITS SOURCE TO ITS MOUTH. IT COLLECTS WATER FROM A VAST AREA OF NORTH-EASTERN AFRICA.

▲Looking across Victoria Nyanza from Kenya. The water looks placid, but Victoria Nyanza is famous for its fierce, sudden tropical storms.

THE NILE HAS TWO ARMS OR BRANCHES. The longer arm is called the White Nile, although its water is usually a muddy grey colour. The source of the White Nile is in the mountains to the west of Victoria Nyanza (Lake Victoria) in the small state of Burundi. Here the river is known as the 'Luvironza'. It flows westwards through the mountains of Burundi until it joins another Nile tributary, the Kagera. This is the largest and longest of the many rivers and streams that empty into Victoria Nyanza. The one river that flows out of Victoria Nyanza is the White Nile.

The second branch of the Nile is the Blue Nile. Its source is above Lake Tana in the mountains of northern Ethiopia. The two Niles meet at Khartoum in Sudan. From there the Nile flows northwards on a winding course across the desert to the Mediterranean Sea. Before it meets the sea, it splits into many creeks, forming a flat, marshy delta. The creeks join to make two channels. They are the Rosetta, on the west of the delta, and the Damietta on the east.

NINE COUNTRIES

The Nile and its tributaries flow through nine countries. The White Nile runs through Uganda, Sudan and Egypt. The Blue Nile

▲ *This false-colour satellite image shows the Nile valley and delta from Aswan northwards. The river banks and the delta (at the top) are reddy-brown. The dark area to the right of the Nile is the Red Sea.*

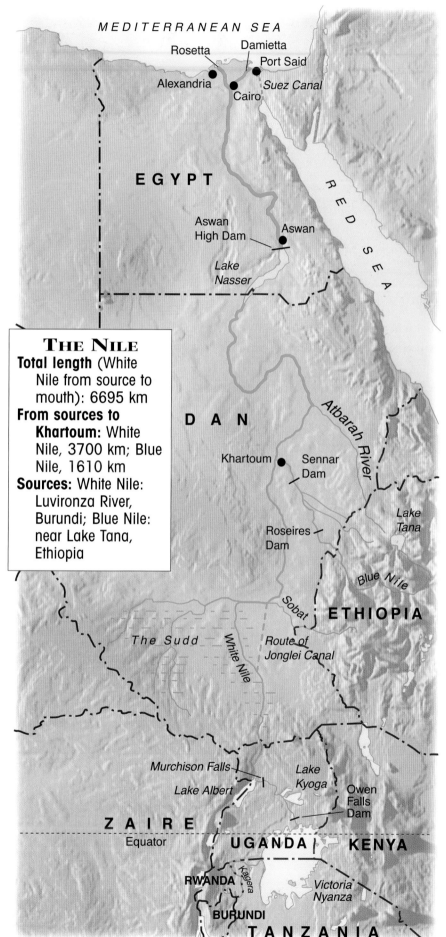

THE NILE
Total length (White Nile from source to mouth): 6695 km
From sources to Khartoum: White Nile, 3700 km; Blue Nile, 1610 km
Sources: White Nile: Luvironza River, Burundi; Blue Nile: near Lake Tana, Ethiopia

starts its journey in Ethiopia. Zaire, Kenya, Tanzania, Rwanda and Burundi have tributaries that flow directly into the Nile or into Victoria Nyanza.

The people of all these countries depend on the Nile as a water supply for themselves and their crops, but none needs the river more than the 82 million people of Egypt. They live in a country that has almost no rainfall, and the Nile must provide all the water they need.

THE MAKING OF THE NILE

THE MOUNTAINOUS AREA WHERE THE WHITE NILE BEGINS IS THE HIGHEST PART OF AFRICA. SOME RIVERS RUN WESTWARDS TO JOIN AFRICA'S SECOND LARGEST RIVER, THE CONGO, WHICH FLOWS INTO THE ATLANTIC OCEAN. OTHERS FLOW NORTH TO FORM THE WHITE NILE.

THE RIFT VALLEY

THE WHITE NILE STARTS ITS JOURNEY through part of the African Rift Valley. There is a series of faults, or cracks, in the Earth's crust. These stretch from the Red Sea in the north to the Zambesi river in southern Africa. Between the fault lines, the land has sunk, forming deep valleys.

One fault line runs to the east of Victoria Nyanza and the Nile. Another, marked by a series of long, narrow, deep lakes, lies to the west and north of Victoria Nyanza. When the White Nile leaves Victoria Nyanza, it flows swiftly between towering cliffs over falls and rapids, finding its way along this second fault line.

Over millions of years, east and west Africa have been slowly pulling apart. One day, in millions of years' time, the break will be complete and the Red Sea will flow into the Rift Valley. This has already happened in the north, where the Red Sea divides Africa from Arabia. Meanwhile, the White Nile makes its way northwards along the western fault to join the faster-flowing Blue Nile at Khartoum.

After the two rivers meet, the Nile flows over a series of long rapids, or cataracts. Then, it meets marshland and desert. After it crosses the border between Sudan and Egypt, it reaches the last stage in its course.

◀ *In the distance are the Blue Mountains of Zaire, which mark the western side of the African Rift Valley.*

> **MAIN TRIBUTARIES OF THE NILE**
> **Kagera**, 691 km; flows into Victoria Nyanza
> **Sobat**, 740 km; joins White Nile at Tawfigiyah, Sudan
> **Atbarah**, 1287 km; joins Nile at Atbarah, Sudan

ACROSS THE DESERT

As the White Nile and Blue Nile pound their way out of the mountains, they bring with them millions of tonnes of soil and fragments of rock. This material is carried along in the fast-flowing water and is joined by more, which the river has washed away from its banks. Until 40 years ago, when the Aswan High Dam was built (see pages 30-31), this material, called sediment, dropped to the river bed or was washed up along the banks. Some of the lighter sediment remained in the water and was carried along until the Nile met the sea. Then this sediment too was deposited. This process, carried on over millions of years, had two effects. It laid a narrow strip of fertile soil no more than about 20 kilometres wide across the Egyptian desert. Then, at the mouth of the Nile, sediments built up a broad delta of flat land jutting out into the Mediterranean. Over 5000 years ago, the fertile strip across the desert and the delta itself became the centre of one of the world's first great civilisations – Ancient Egypt.

▲The Blue Nile in Ethiopia as it begins its 1610-kilometre journey to meet the White Nile at Khartoum in Sudan.

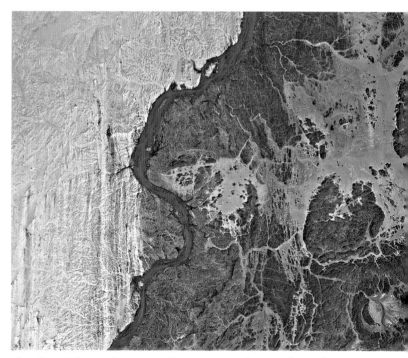

▲ This false-colour satellite image shows the Nile running through the Nubian Desert in Sudan. On the right is the hilly landscape and on the left is sand. The river is the only source of water in this area - the only patches of vegetation are in red.

ANCIENT EGYPT

THE FOUNDERS OF ANCIENT EGYPT DISCOVERED THE VALLEY OF THE LOWER NILE ABOUT 10,000 YEARS AGO. BY ABOUT 5000 BC THEY WERE FARMING THE LAND BY THE RIVER AND USING THE WATER FOR THEIR CROPS.

BY ABOUT 3250 BC EGYPT was split into two kingdoms. Lower Egypt was on the Nile delta. Its capital was Buto near the present-day city of Damanhur. Upper Egypt was in the Nile valley and was ruled from Hierakonopolis, on the opposite bank of the Nile to today's El Kab. By this time there were towns and villages dotted along the river banks as far upstream as present-day Aswan.

In about 3100 BC the more powerful Upper Egyptian ruler, Menes, conquered Lower Egypt and the two kingdoms became one.

Menes built a new capital city at Memphis, close to where the Nile valley opens out to form the delta. This was the start of the civilisation of Ancient Egypt, with its pyramids, temples and palaces.

▲ From about 1500 BC to 343 BC, the Ancient Egyptian empire stretched south along the Nile through Nubia, now part of Sudan.

▼ An Egyptian rests with his camel in front of the Step Pyramid at Saqqara, built in about 2660 BC.

▼ *An ox-driven waterwheel, a saqqiya, built to the same design as the Egyptians used in the last centuries* BC. *The ox pulls round the horizontal cogwheel, which then drives the vertical wheel. This operates a chain of jugs, which lift up water from an irrigation canal.*

▲ *This wall-painting in the tomb of Sennedjem shows Sennedjem and his wife ploughing, sowing seed and reaping in the Fields of Iaru, the Ancient Egyptian Afterworld.*

THE AGE OF THE PYRAMIDS

In the next 1500 years many of the famous monuments of Ancient Egypt were built. They include the earliest stone pyramid to have survived, the Step Pyramid at Saqqara. The Ancient Egyptians buried their kings in the pyramids with all their favourite possessions, such as fine clothes, furniture and jewellery. They also left food and drink for the king's journey to the next world.

There are over 100 pyramids in Egypt and Sudan, a country which became part of the Ancient Egyptian empire. The Egyptians also left behind many other fine buildings, including huge statues and temples of their kings and gods. The Egyptians excelled at pottery, metalwork and weaving, and enjoyed music and dancing. They developed a system of picture-writing called hieroglyphs. They

discovered how to make a kind of paper out of a reed called papyrus, which grew along the banks of the Nile. The Egyptians were also great warriors. At its height, in about 1500 BC, their empire stretched down the eastern coast of the Mediterranean through present-day Israel and Lebanon and south into Sudan.

THE ANCIENT EGYPTIAN EMPIRE

Egypt's wealth came from the rich harvests of the fertile soil of the Nile valley and delta. Grain was exchanged abroad for timber, Silver and other goods that Egypt did not have. The Ancient Egyptian empire lasted for about 2500 years, far longer than any other empire in history. It came to an end in 343 BC when the last Egyptian Pharaoh, Nectanebo II, died.

THE ANNUAL FLOOD

FROM ASWAN TO THE NILE DELTA, A DISTANCE OF 1000 KILOMETRES, THE NILE VALLEY IS ALMOST LEVEL. UNTIL THE 1960S, THE NILE OVERFLOWED ON TO THE LAND EVERY JUNE.

THE AVERAGE RISE IN THE WATER level was eight metres. It was October before the water drained away to the sea, leaving behind swamps and pools that slowly dried up in the sun. The flood waters also left behind some of the sediment they had brought down from the mountains. Thousands of years of annual flooding gave the narrow strip of the lower Nile Valley a top layer of rich, black soil as fertile as any land in the world. On each side of this strip the desert closed in, hot, dry and lifeless.

THE RAINY SEASON

The White Nile, which collects its water from the mountains and tropical rainforests of central Africa, has a fairly even flow of water throughout the year. The lakes along its course, such as Victoria Nyanza and Lake Kyoga in Uganda, act as natural reservoirs for the water draining into them. They release this water in a steady flow, which prevents the lower Nile from drying up even in the dry season.

▼ *Before the Aswan High Dam was built, these fields were flooded every summer. Now that the dam holds back the flood, a network of irrigation canals brings water to the crops.*

▲*Storm clouds gather over the mountains in Ethiopia.*

THE NILE CALENDAR

The water level in the Blue Nile begins to rise in June, and by July the flood has reached Aswan. It rises quickly in August and reaches its peak at Aswan at the beginning of September. After that, the flood begins to die away.

PREDICTABLE FLOODS

As far as historians and scientists can tell, the Nile's annual flood has never failed to arrive, although some years it is smaller than others. Neither has it ever threatened life by coming early or by being unusually heavy. The time of its arrival varies by no more than three weeks. Other floods on the world's great rivers, like the Yangtze in China or the Ganges in Bangladesh, are less reliable. Sometimes their floods do not arrive as expected, bringing starvation to millions of people. Sometimes they come at the same time as fierce tropical storms, whipping up the floodwater and causing great damage and loss of life. But the Nile's flood was so regular that a whole ancient civilisation lasting thousands of years was based on its annual rise and fall.

▼*The water near the source of the Blue Nile rises as rainstorms close in across Ethiopia. This is the start of the Nile's flood season.*

The Blue Nile's water level changes greatly through the seasons. Every year in early summer, storms sweep in from the Indian Ocean across the mountains of Ethiopia where the Blue Nile has its source.

Torrential rain adds to the water already pouring off the mountains as the snow melts. The Blue Nile, hurtling down through deep gorges and over rapids, tears at loose rocks and soil and carries them along with it. The force of the current scours more material up from the river bed. The usually clear water turns brown because of this sediment as it joins the White Nile at Khartoum and flows north towards Egypt.

TALES OF THE NILE

GODS, KINGS AND QUEENS ARE THE HEROES AND HEROINES
OF MANY OF THE STORIES OF THE NILE.

RA THE SUN GOD AND SET THE EVIL

THE ANCIENT EGYPTIANS believed that their rulers were gods, and all citizens were children of the great god Ra, the sun-god. Ra sailed over the Earth by day in his boat, and travelled under the Earth by night. His deadly enemy was Set the Evil.

The god of the Nile was Osiris, who was murdered by Set. Osiris had a son, Horus, who set out to avenge his father's death. Borrowing Ra's boat, he sailed up the Nile to where Set had camped on an island near Aswan. When Set saw Horus coming, he caused a great storm, which tossed Ra's boat about on mighty waves. But Horus held on, calling on Ra to help him.

Ra put a heavy chain in Horus's hands and made the waves still so that Horus could throw the chain around Set and bind him tightly. Horus sailed with his captive to Thebes, Ra's sacred city.

There, Set was put on trial and condemned to live underground in a cave forever. Then Ra proclaimed Horus king of Egypt.

THE QUEEN OF SHEBA

Axum is a town in northern Ethiopia, close to the Takazze river which later joins the Atbarah tributary of the Nile. According to legend, in the tenth century BC Axum was the capital of Ethiopia under the rule of the Queen of Sheba. A large ruined building in the town is said to have been her palace, and a stone column nearby marks her grave.

The Queen of Sheba ruled at the same time as Solomon, king of Israel, who was famous for his wisdom. The Queen led a camel-train 2400 kilometres to meet Solomon in Jerusalem, taking with her gifts of gold, precious stones and spices. She later had Solomon's child, Menelik.

Solomon built a temple in Jerusalem to house the most sacred Jewish religious object, a chest called the 'Ark of the Covenant'. It later disappeared. Ethiopians say that Menelik brought it to Axum, where he became king after his mother's death. A chapel in the town is still said to contain the Ark, but no visitors are ever allowed to check this claim.

◀ *About 3000 years ago, the Queen of Sheba ruled over Ethiopia as well as southern Arabia, which was only 27 kilometres away across the Red Sea.*

QUEEN HATSHEPSUT'S FLEET

▼Queen Hatshepsut's temple near Thebes, cut from the rock of the cliffs behind it. The temple was built as her mortuary temple and to celebrate the events of her reign as Queen of Egypt from 1503 BC to 1484 BC. Sweet-smelling myrhh trees were brought back after the expedition to Punt. They lined the approach to the temple.

In 1503 BC, a princess called Hatshepsut became Queen of Egypt. The temple built for her near Thebes, which is still there, contains wall-reliefs telling stories of her reign. One story is of a great expedition she organised to a land that the Egyptians called 'Punt'. This is now thought to be Somalia.

A special fleet of eight ships was built. It set off in 1492 BC laden with gifts for the ruler of Punt. The Egyptians were not used to long sea journeys and it must have been a frightening voyage, especially as the sailors were heading for an unknown land. But they were received kindly and returned to Egypt with cargoes of incense, perfume and animal skins. One relief in Queen Hatshepsut's temple shows her welcoming the sailors home and watching the treasures being weighed.

THE SEARCH FOR THE SOURCE

EGYPT AND THE LOWER NILE VALLEY HAVE BEEN PART OF THE KNOWN WORLD FOR THOUSANDS OF YEARS, BUT THE LAND BEYOND THE MEETING OF THE WHITE AND BLUE NILES WAS UNKNOWN TO OUTSIDERS UNTIL ABOUT 200 YEARS AGO.

DIFFICULT COUNTRY, fierce heat, tropical diseases, wild animals and attacks by hostile tribes all put off travellers. The source of the Blue Nile was discovered in 1770 by a Scottish explorer, James Bruce. But the source of the White Nile remained a mystery for almost another 100 years.

MOUNTAINS OF THE MOON

Travellers from Ancient Egypt reached as far upstream as the present site of Khartoum, the meeting place of the two Niles, but went no further. In about AD 60, when Egypt had become part of the Roman empire, the Emperor Nero sent an expedition southwards to find the Nile's source. The explorers returned without success. Their way had been blocked by the Sudd – a swampy area of tangled, floating plants and trees.

At the same time, a Greek merchant named Diogenes reported a journey he had made inland from the east coast of Africa. He had seen two great lakes and a range of snowy mountains that he thought must contain the source of the Nile. The Greek-Egyptian geographer Ptolemy used this and other travellers' tales to draw a map of the Nile in the second century AD. This shows the river rising in a great lake at the foot of what he called the 'Mountains of the Moon'.

◄ *The Mountains of the Moon, Ruwenzori, in western Uganda. The huge shrub in the foreground is a giant lobelia.*

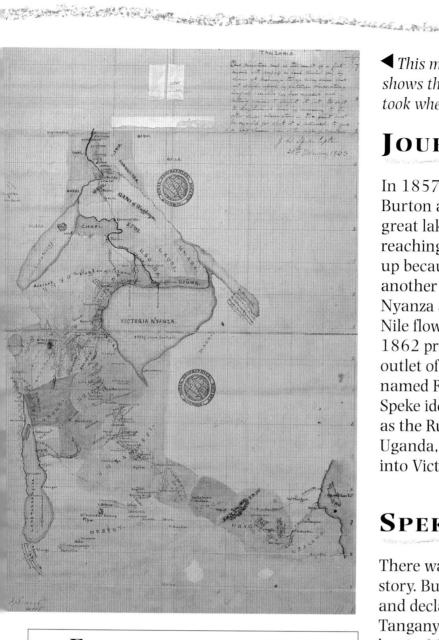

◀ *This map was drawn by Grant in 1863 and it shows the route (marked in pink) he and Speke took when searching for the source of the Nile.*

JOURNEY OF DISCOVERY

In 1857, a British expedition led by Richard Burton and John Speke set out to find the great lakes shown on Ptolemy's map. After reaching Lake Tanganyika, the two men split up because Burton was ill. Travelling on for another month, Speke discovered Victoria Nyanza and was convinced that the White Nile flowed from it. A second expedition in 1862 proved him right when he found the outlet of the Nile at a waterfall which he named Ripon Falls. On the same expedition, Speke identified the 'Mountains of the Moon' as the Ruwenzori Mountains in western Uganda, from which the Katonga river flows into Victoria Nyanza.

SPEKE'S END

There was a strange and tragic end to Speke's story. Burton refused to accept Speke's ideas and declared that the Nile flowed from Lake Tanganyika. The two men quarrelled bitterly, but in 1864 they agreed to argue the case in public. But on the day before the debate was due to take place, Speke went out shooting partridges and accidentally shot himself dead. An expedition led by Henry Morton Stanley in 1875 proved that Speke was right.

EXPLORERS ON THE NILE

1769: James Bruce. Reached the source of the Blue Nile in November 1770.

1857: Richard Burton and John Speke. Reached Lake Tanganyika in February 1858. Speke travelled on and reached Victoria Nyanza in March 1858.

1860: John Speke and James Grant. Reached Victoria Nyanza in July 1862 and discovered and named the Ripon Falls. Travelled down the White Nile to Gondokoro in southern Sudan.

1861: Samuel and Florence White Baker. Travelled up the Nile and met Speke and Grant at Gondokoro in February 1865. Discovered and named Lake Albert.

1874: Henry Morton Stanley. Sailed round Victoria Nyanza in April 1875 and confirmed that the Nile's outlet was at the Ripon Falls.

▶ *John Speke was 30 when he began his first expedition in Africa.*

VICTORIA NYANZA

VICTORIA NYANZA COVERS AN AREA OF 69,500 SQUARE KILOMETRES — ABOUT THREE TIMES THE SIZE OF WALES. IT IS THE SECOND LARGEST FRESHWATER LAKE IN THE WORLD.

THE NILE LEAVES VICTORIA NYANZA through a single outlet on the north coast near Jinja. This outlet, discovered by Speke and Grant in 1862, was the Ripon Falls, a 275-metre wide waterfall divided into three channels by two wooded islands. The Ripon Falls have now disappeared under the reservoir of the Owen Falls Dam downstream, but the Nile still flows through the same gap in the rocks.

▼*The White Nile leaves Victoria Nyanza through the Owen Falls Dam, built in the 1950s to provide hydro-electric power for Uganda's capital, Kampala.*

SHALLOW LAKE

Victoria Nyanza stands on a plateau of high ground between the two faults of the African Rift Valley. It is a shallow lake, only about 82 metres deep at its deepest point, and in many

▶ *These fishermen have caught Nile perch on Victoria Nyanza. The lake is an important source for the local fishing industry and an important means of transport.*

VICTORIA NYANZA
Greatest length: 400 km
Greatest width: 320 km
Greatest depth: 82 m
Length of coastline: 3220 km
Height above sea level:
    1134 m

places there are reefs just below the surface of the water that are dangerous to ships. Lake Tanganyika to the west follows the Rift Valley and is one of the deepest lakes in the world – up to 1400 metres in places.

A MAGNET FOR PEOPLE

Compared with other parts of inland Africa, the area round Victoria Nyanza is densely populated. About 40 million people live within about 300 kilometres of the lake, either around the shores or in the highlands behind them. There are two rainy seasons, which give good growing conditions for crops such as coffee and cotton for export and maize for home use. But in some places in the hills on the south and east sides of the lake, the land has been damaged by over-cultivation and soil erosion. When the land has been exhausted and all its natural chemicals have been used up, farmers often abandon it and move on. They 'slash and burn' woodland to clear new areas for planting. On slopes, this results in the top soil being washed away by rain into the rivers and streams.

▲ *'Slash and burn' cultivation in Uganda. The trees are cleared and used for fuel, and the roots and undergrowth are burned. Rain washes the ash into the soil where it acts as a fertiliser. This plot of land will produce good crops for three or four seasons before it becomes exhausted.*

THE WHITE NILE

THE WHITE NILE IS THE NAME USUALLY GIVEN TO THE STRETCH OF
RIVER BETWEEN VICTORIA NYANZA AND KHARTOUM. THE NAME
COMES FROM THE MILKY-WHITE COLOUR OF THE WATER AS THE
RIVER FLOWS THROUGH SUDAN IN THE SUMMER.

YOU MAY FIND OTHER NAMES for the White Nile on maps and in
atlases. One African name is 'Kir'. The Sudanese call it 'Bahr
al Abyad' (the White River) between Khartoum and the
meeting of the Sobat river with the Nile, and 'Bahr al Jabal'
(the Mountain River) for the length upstream through Sudan.
Nineteenth-century British explorers gave the name 'Victoria
Nile' to the section from Victoria Nyanza to Lake Albert, and
'Albert Nile' between Lake Albert and the border between
Uganda and Sudan. Albert was the name of Queen Victoria's
husband, the Prince Consort.

▼*The White Nile pours over
the Murchison Falls in north-
western Uganda on its way to
Lake Albert. The two separate
torrents can be clearly seen.*

FALLS AND RAPIDS

After the White Nile leaves Victoria Nyanza, it races through
the mountains between cliffs that are up to 55 metres high,

over a series of spectacular falls and rapids. After about 112 kilometres the river enters a shallow lake, Lake Kyoga, with swamps at its edges. It seems to pause before plunging again between rocks and thundering over the Murchison Falls, which are 40 metres high.

The Murchison Falls provide an example of how rivers can change. When they were discovered in 1864 by Samuel White Baker, the first European to see them, the river poured through a gap of only six metres. But in 1961 unusually heavy rain brought floods which broke through the rocks at a second point so that the Murchison Falls now consist of two separate torrents.

Changing course

The pattern of rapid descent followed by slower waters is repeated several times along the White Nile. Lake Kyoga, Lake Albert and some smaller lakes help to regulate the flow of water, which explains why the White Nile flows more evenly than the Blue Nile. Below

Lake Albert, the water again speeds up over a series of rapids as it crosses the border from Uganda into Sudan. This area of mountains, lakes and deep gorges is the home of many animals. Crocodiles lurk in the quiet patches of water, where hippopotamus bathe. Elephants, buffalo, giraffes and several species of antelope also inhabit this region, which is now one of Uganda's national wildlife parks.

▼ *A hippopotamus takes a curious look at a passing Nile cruiser. Hippos live in herds of 20 to 40 on the river banks, but they spend most of their time in the river where they feed on water plants.*

The lakes of the White Nile
Lake Kyoga, Uganda
    Greatest length: 137 km
    Greatest width: 16 km
    Greatest depth: 6 m
Lake Albert, Zaire/Uganda
    Greatest length: 160 km
    Greatest width: 35 km
    Greatest depth: 16.5 m

◄ *Fishermen at work in the quieter waters below Murchison Falls. The Falls are the focal point of one of Uganda's national parks.*

THROUGH THE SWAMPS

EARLY EXPLORERS TRAVELLING UP THE WHITE NILE
FOUND THEIR WAY BLOCKED BY A GREAT SWAMP.
THIS IS CALLED THE 'SUDD'.

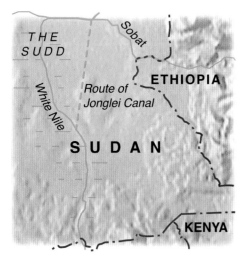

THE SUDD IS A SOLID MASS of ferns, reeds and other rotting vegetation. It stretches for about 650 kilometres south from the point where the Sobat river joins the Nile.

'THIS HORRIBLE REGION'

The Sudd has been formed by the action of the river over thousands of years. Each year the river brings down more floating vegetation, and the current packs it solid. In places, the vegetation is six metres deep and solid enough to support the weight of an elephant. From time to time, blocks of the Sudd break away and form floating islands until they are caught on another obstruction. Closely packed reeds and grasses rise up to five metres above the water. In the wet season, the Sudd covers an area the size of England.

The explorer Samuel White Baker wrote in 1866 that 'some evil spirit appears to rule in this horrible region of everlasting swamp'. The hot, humid air, the smell of rotting vegetation and the clouds of mosquitoes and other insects make it one of the

PEOPLE OF THE SUDD

The Sudd itself contains no resources to support human life and is uninhabited, but small groups of herding families live at its edges. They graze their animals and grow a little grain on grassland that is flooded each year by the White Nile. These families are members of three closely-related peoples, the Nuer, the Dinka and the Shilluk tribes. Because they live in such a remote region, and also because they have avoided contact with the few travellers they might see, little is known about them. Each group is ruled by a chief whose main duty is to pray for rain.

▶ Balaeniceps rex, *the whale-headed stork or shoebill, is one of the rare species that live in the Sudd. Standing about 1.5 metres tall, its scowling eyes and hugh hooked beak give it a grim appearance.*

most unpleasant environments on Earth. No one can live there. Travellers face an unbearable climate and the likelihood of fever and sunstroke.

THE JONGLEI PROJECT

As well as preventing navigation up the White Nile, the Sudd has a serious effect on the flow of the river downstream. In the fierce heat, the water flowing slowly through the swamp evaporates. This loss of river water is serious for northern Sudan.

Plans were made in the early 1950s to cut a canal round the Sudd, in the Jonglei region, to speed up the flow of water so that less would evaporate. There was to be a main canal that would take about half the Nile's water, while a second canal would be used for local irrigation projects. But in 1955 civil war broke out between north and south Sudan and lasted for seventeen years. When it was over, the Jonglei

plans were revived. A giant German digger called the 'Bucketwheel' was brought in and in the early 1980s work began on the main canal. Over 260 kilometres – most of the planned length – had been cut when civil war broke out again in 1984 and work had to stop. The main canal was only a year away from completion. The Bucketwheel is still there today, silent and rusting.

Meanwhile, the banks and bed of the canal have dried out and crumbled. The irrigation canal that would have provided much-needed food crops for Sudan was never started. It will be hard for the Sudanese government to persuade international banks and aid agencies to lend them money to finish the project.

▼ *The giant 'Bucketwheel' digger stands abandoned when work on the Jonglei Canal stopped in 1984. The French engineering team who were digging the canal had to leave when they were attacked by Sudanese rebels.*

THE SUDANESE NILE

AFTER THE WHITE NILE FLOWS THROUGH THE SUDD, IT MOVES ON ACROSS SUDAN OVER AN AREA OF DRY GRASSLAND TOWARDS KHARTOUM, WHERE THE BLUE NILE JOINS IT FROM THE EAST.

SUDAN IS THE LARGEST COUNTRY in Africa, covering over 2.5 million square kilometres. This is about a quarter of the area of Europe. Most of its 40 million people live close to the Nile.

THE SPREADING DESERT

The southern Sudanese people make a poor living from farming and cattle-rearing. Many people are nomadic, moving about with their herds in search of fresh grazing and water. Over the past 30 years this search has become more difficult across a broad band of central Sudan. Long periods of drought since the 1960s have allowed the Sahara desert to spread southwards. Farmland became useless for crops as duststorms blew the thin top soil away and sand took its place. The land around remaining wells and waterholes became overgrazed as herds of animals gathered round them.

▶ *Herdsmen bring their goats to a waterhole in the Sudanese desert while other herds wait their turn. The demand for grazing vegetation and water is intense. As the Sahara desert spreads, more herds are forced to use a declining number of oases and waterholes and to feed on a smaller area of grazing land. Some Sudanese herdsmen and their families give up the struggle to keep their animals alive and healthy and head for cities like Khartoum where they join thousands already searching for work and homes.*

The southern Sudanese have come to realise that people in the north of their country have easier, more prosperous lives. This is the main cause of the civil wars that have raged between north and south for over 40 years, broken by short periods of peace. The southerners were against the Jonglei project and attacked its workers. They thought that finding a way for the Nile to go round the Sudd would only benefit the north by providing a better flow of water for irrigation. There are also religious differences between the north and south. People in the north are mainly Muslim. In the south the people have older religious beliefs going back deep into African tribal history.

WHERE THE RIVERS MEET

The Blue Nile meets the White Nile at Khartoum on the southern edge of the Nubian Desert.

Khartoum and its two neighbouring cities,

POPULATION GROWTH IN SUDAN			
	1925	1980	1995
Sudan	6m	17m	30m
Khartoum/ Khartoum North	45,000	784,000	3m
Omdurman	78,000	526,000	635,000

Khartoum North and Omdurman, make a triangle on each bank of the two Niles. They are the centre of Sudan's government, trade, transport system and industry. The poverty in most of the rest of Sudan makes them a magnet for families hoping to find work, and the three cities are growing rapidly.

▼*Omdurman, on the west bank of the Nile opposite Khartoum, is Sudan's main trading city. The minarets dominating the skyline show the importance of Islam, which has been the main religion of northern Sudan for 500 years.*

THE BLUE NILE

THE BLUE NILE IS THE SOURCE OF MOST OF THE FLOODWATER THAT GIVES EGYPT LIFE. ALTHOUGH IT IS LESS THAN HALF AS LONG AS THE WHITE NILE, IN THE RAINY SEASON IT CARRIES FOUR TIMES AS MUCH WATER.

LIKE THE WHITE NILE, the Blue Nile starts life as a mountain stream. It is called the Little Abbai and flows to Lake Tana, 112 kilometres away.

FORESTS AND FALLS

Leaving the lake, the Blue Nile soon plunges through rockpools and rapids until it reaches the Tisisat Falls, where its waters pour over a 46-metre drop. This is the start of a huge curve which takes the river round three-quarters of a circle through the Gojam

▼ Beaten earth bricks, dried grasses, reeds, and corrugated iron are used to build this Ethiopian village close to the Nile. The hut on the right, which is being re-roofed, shows how the roof is made.

▶ *The Blue Nile looks peaceful as it leaves Lake Tana in Ethiopia, but soon it will begin its furious journey over rapids and falls as it escapes from the Gojam Mountains.*

Mountains. On the way it passes through the Blue Nile Gorge, which is 1.6 kilometres deep and about the same distance across, where the river flows between sheer cliff faces.

Leaving the mountains behind, the Blue Nile flows past small villages of cone-shaped grass huts. The villagers live mainly on maize, but they eat fish or antelope meat from time to time. The women fetch their water from the river in gourds, which are the empty rinds of giant fruit. The way of life in these villages, cut off by poor communications, has changed little over thousands of years.

THE GEZIRA SCHEME

The Gezira scheme was begun in the 1920s when the Sennar Dam was built. It is one of the largest irrigation schemes on the Nile.

This scheme holds back and stores some of the Blue Nile's seasonal floodwater, which is released into a canal running parallel to the river. The canal irrigates an area of land between the rivers about 320 kilometres long by 100 kilometres wide. Cotton and wheat are the main crops here. In the 1960s the Gezira scheme was extended when a second dam was built at Roseires, together with a power station to provide electricity for the cities at the junction of the two Niles.

◀ *A young field-worker picks cotton in the Gezira area. Cotton is a 'cash crop', which farmers can sell to help support their families.*

THE ASWAN HIGH DAM

THE BIGGEST SINGLE CHANGE ON THE NILE IN ALL ITS HISTORY WAS THE BUILDING OF THE ASWAN HIGH DAM IN EGYPT. IT TOOK TEN YEARS TO BUILD AND WAS COMPLETED IN 1970.

THE ASWAN HIGH DAM is 114 metres high and 3.6 kilometres long. Upstream, it creates a reservoir of water, called Lake Nasser, which stretches back for 270 kilometres into northern Sudan. Before the reservoir was made, the land was the home of 100,000 farming people who had to be given new houses and land, irrigated from the lake, above the new water level.

CONTROLLING THE FLOOD

The most important change that the Aswan High Dam brought about was that it made the annual flooding of the Nile valley in Egypt a thing of the past. The floodwaters are now trapped in Lake Nasser behind the dam, and their flow

▲Technicians at Abu Simbel supervise the removal of the head of Rameses II, who had the temple built in about 1270 BC.

▶ The re-sited temple of Abu Simbel above Lake Nasser.

◀ *One of the hydro-electric generators on the Aswan High Dam. The dam was built in the 1960s with money and technical help from the former Soviet Union.*

Egypt's other urgent need as its leaders tried to modernise the country – energy. By the 1980s, the generators driven by water flowing through the dam were providing half of Egypt's electricity, but by the 1990s this proportion had fallen as energy demands grew.

PLUS AND MINUS

The Aswan High Dam was a successful project, giving Egypt and northern Sudan extra farmland and providing electricity for Egyptian cities. Lake Nasser has created a flourishing fishing industry, which produces 25,000 tonnes of fish a year and has a target of 100,000 tonnes by the year 2000.

But some other results of the project are not so good. Sediment from the Nile is held back behind the dam, and experts say that over the next 100 years Lake Nasser will steadily fill with silt. If this happens, the water level would rise and the lake would overflow, making new irrigation work urgently necessary. Some experts even fear that the weight of sediment could eventually break the dam, which would bring major disaster to Egypt, with huge damage and loss of life. Meanwhile, as much as ten per cent of the water flowing into Lake Nasser is lost through evaporation into the dry, hot air. This is water Egypt cannot afford to lose. In the valley below Aswan, the dam has altered the Egyptians' traditional way of farming.

The building of the High Dam solved some of Egypt's immediate problems, but may have stored up others for the future.

into the valley can be controlled. This has enabled more land in the valley to be irrigated, partly to feed Egypt's growing population, which doubled from 14 to 28 million between 1925 and 1950. (It had doubled again by 1995 and is expected to reach 68 million by the year 2000.) Egypt also needed more land for crops that could be exported, such as cotton and fruit.

The High Dam was also designed to meet

THE GREAT TEMPLE AT ABU SIMBEL

Raising the water level at Aswan drowned many of the monuments of Ancient Egypt, but some were saved. Among these was the Great Temple at Abu Simbel, built around 1300 BC as a monument to King Rameses II. Four colossi, or statues, of the king show him as a sun-god, surrounded by his wife, mother and children. The figures of the king are between eighteen and twenty metres tall. Between 1964 and 1968, the temple and its statues were sawn into blocks and rebuilt on a new site 65 metres above and 210 metres away from the old one. The work was supervised by the world's leading experts on Ancient Egypt.

THE NILE VALLEY

BEFORE THE ASWAN HIGH DAM WAS BUILT, LIFE IN THE FARMING SETTLEMENTS OF THE NILE VALLEY HAD HARDLY ALTERED OVER HUNDREDS OF YEARS. NOW, THINGS ARE CHANGING.

EGYPTIAN CROPS

	tonnes (1995)
Cane sugar	11.9 million
Maize (corn)	4.9 million
Rice	4.5 million
Wheat	4.4 million
Vegetables	10.8 million
Fruit	3.8 million
Cotton	314 thousand

▼ *A village beside an irrigation canal in the Nile Valley. The land is divided between cash crops and food crops for the village families. The concrete structure on the canal bank is a sluice which can be opened to let water flow to the fields beyond.*

RELEASING FLOODWATER through the Aswan High Dam steadily throughout the year instead of relying on the annual flood has increased the area of land that can be irrigated and farmed. The cotton crop, for example, has increased by 30 per cent since 1970. But because sediment is trapped by the dam, farmers in the valley can no longer rely on the Nile to deposit natural mineral salts to feed their crops. The soil of the valley is becoming less fertile. So they have to buy chemical fertilisers which, as well as being expensive, seep into the irrigation canals and pollute them. Egypt uses an average of one-quarter of a tonne of chemicals on each hectare of land, one of the highest usage levels in the world.

UPGRADING IRRIGATION

The new conditions after the building of the dam alerted Egyptians to how much water was being wasted. Many of the

main irrigation canals in the valley were at least 200 years old. They had not been well-maintained and were in poor condition. A project was started to upgrade over 30,000 kilometres of the irrigation system by repairing banks and lining the canal beds with concrete to stop water seeping away. The improved water supply enabled more irrigation works to be carried out and more land to be brought into use for farming. Since the dam was built, the area of farmland in the valley has increased by 25 per cent. But with Egypt's ever-growing population to be fed, there are plans to widen the farming land (see pages 42-43) still further.

LIFE IN THE VILLAGES

The modernisation of Egypt since about 1960 has brought great benefits to the people of the Nile villages. Before then, they drank water from the river and the canals, which were also used as sewers. The result was continual outbreaks of water-borne diseases such as bilharzia. This disease is carried by water-snails and enters the bloodstream through grazes on the skin. Today, almost all except the most remote villages have a clean, piped water supply, and disease is much less common.

One tradition, thousands of years old, has gone for ever since the High Dam was built. Villagers in the valley used to build their homes with mud-bricks cut and shaped on the river bank and left to dry in the sun. Today, not enough silt comes down to the valley to be spared for brick-making, and modern homes are made from factory-baked sand bricks that are more expensive.

▲ This mud-brick village is approximately 20 kilometres north of the town of Aswan and only a few hundred metres from the Nile. Many of the houses have electricity supplied by the Aswan High Dam.

◀ Water levels in the Nile are controlled by barrages like this one at Esna towards the northern end of te valley. The amount of water flowing through is controlled from the overhead gantry.

CITIES OF THE DELTA

EGYPT

FOR THE LAST 150 KILOMETRES OF ITS COURSE TO THE MEDITERRANEAN SEA, THE NILE FANS OUT ACROSS A DELTA, WHICH, AT THE COAST, IS ABOUT 150 KILOMETRES WIDE. THE CITIES OF THE DELTA MAKE IT ONE OF THE MOST DENSELY POPULATED AREAS IN THE WORLD, WITH 1000 PEOPLE TO EACH SQUARE KILOMETRE.

CAIRO, EGYPT'S CAPITAL at the southern head of the delta, is Africa's largest city with a population of over fifteen million. Another five million people travel into Cairo every day to work. Alexandria, with four million people, is Egypt's second largest city and its main port. Both cities are badly overcrowded, with transport, housing and services such as

▼ *Cairo has swallowed up good farming land that Egypt desperately needs.*

sewage under huge strain. Neither city was designed to house so many people.

NEW CITIES

Improvements are slowly being made in Cairo. New roads are being constructed and the entire city's water supply, which includes a recycling scheme to prevent waste, is being rebuilt. But the real answer is to stop the

◄ *A container ship on the Suez Canal. Between 1976 and 1980 the canal was enlarged to keep pace with the increasing size of modern shipping.*

POPULATION (2006)	
National population: 72.5 million	
Cairo: 15.8 million	
Alexandria: 4 million	
Port Said: 571,000	
Ismailia: 943,000	
Mahalla: 442,000	
Helwan: 643,000	
Port Suez: 511,000	

city's growth and rehouse many of its people in new towns on the edges of the delta. The Egyptian government plans to build offices and factories in these new towns to take the pressure off Cairo and Alexandria. Four new towns – Sadat City, Salam City, Fifteenth of May City and Sixth of October City – are already being built.

The delta is the home of Egypt's main industries. Mahalla, north of Cairo, is a textile city. It began as a centre for spinning and weaving Egyptian cotton, but today it also produces synthetic fibres and cloth using the products of Egypt's growing petro-chemical industry. Helwan, to the south of Cairo, is an iron and steel manufacturing city. As well as producing raw iron and steel, it also makes domestic appliances, car parts and electronic equipment.

THE SUEZ CANAL

To the east of the Nile delta, the Suez Canal links the Mediterranean Sea and the Red Sea. It was opened in 1869 and is a vital link for shipping between Europe and the Far East, as it cuts out the long voyage around the southern tip of Africa. Widened and deepened for modern shipping, the Suez Canal is 173 kilometres long, at least 200 metres wide and 20 metres deep. An average of 90 ships a day pass through it, from Port Said on the Mediterranean to Port Suez on the Red Sea. They take about fifteen hours for the journey because their speed is restricted to avoid too much 'wash' that would damage the banks. The fees the ships pay are an important source of income for Egypt.

▲ *A false-colour satellite image of the Nile delta highlighting particular features. The blue-grey area next to the yellow is Cairo. The red area shows cultivated land. Here the two main outlets of the Nile, the Rosetta and the Damietta, can be seen. The thin line on the right is the Suez Canal.*

SHARING THE WATERS

THERE ARE NINE COUNTRIES ON THE NILE OR ITS TRIBUTARIES,
BUT FOUR OF THEM — EGYPT, SUDAN, ETHIOPIA AND
UGANDA — HOLD THE KEY TO ITS FUTURE.

EGYPT IS ENTIRELY DEPENDENT on the Nile for water. Its government has said that if any of the other Nile countries tried to interfere with its supply it would go to war. There is an agreement with Sudan about how much water each country takes from the river, but no agreement exists with the other countries. Sudan too needs more water for irrigation. But it is Ethiopia that controls the source of the Blue Nile, and the White Nile flows out of Victoria Nyanza in Uganda.

DEVELOPING ETHIOPIA

Egypt is concerned about future developments in Ethiopia, a country whose development has been held up by years of civil war. But now the war is over, the country wants to catch up on development. It is desperately short of farmland. Desertification and the clearing of forests for firewood - Ethiopia's main source of energy for cooking and heating - have led to an urgent need for irrigation schemes and hydro-electricity. The country faces a huge population growth, from 60 million in 1995 to an estimated 70 million by the year 2000. There is already not enough land to feed the population.

The Blue Nile contributes about 80 per cent of the water that reaches Egypt. The Ethiopians watch this water flow by, but they receive little benefit from it. The Ethiopian government has a plan to build 26 dams for irrigation and electricity generation on the Blue Nile and its tributaries. For Egypt and Sudan, this would be a disaster. It would result in a 20 per cent loss of Nile water for Egypt. At the moment, Ethiopia cannot afford to go ahead with its plan, but it is trying to obtain loans and technical help from other countries. If it went ahead without Egypt's agreement, there would be a major war in north-east Africa. It is very unlikely that Egypt would agree to the building of the dams.

◀ *The Nile supplies the water needs of many different peoples. These Ugandan people are coming back from the river with their supplies.*

▶ *Intensely cultivated fields press up against the city of Luxor in the Nile valley. The future of such prosperous scenes depends on the continued flow of the Nile.*

THE KEY NILE COUNTRIES		
	Population 1995	2000 estimate
Egypt	62 million	68 million
Sudan	30 million	34 million
Ethiopia	60 million	70 million
Uganda	19 million	21 million

WATER AND ENERGY

Experts believe that there is a solution. They say that the Nile could be harnessed, if all nine countries agreed, to provide enough water and electricity for all. Ethiopia could continue to let the Blue Nile flow down to Sudan and Egypt in return for electricity. Uganda could build new dams on the White Nile to provide a supply of water and electricity which could be piped downstream. These projects would be costly, involving the building of pipelines and electricity grids, and they would need international help. But they would allow the Nile countries to share its resources in peace.

▼ *A sugar-cane plantation in Sudan, irrigated by the Blue Nile. Sudan needs more irrigated land for cash crops and to feed its growing population.*

THE NILE'S WILDLIFE

THE NILE FLOWS THROUGH EVERY KIND OF TROPICAL ENVIRONMENT FROM DESERT AND SEMI-DESERT TO RAINFOREST. AS HUMAN SETTLEMENT HAS INCREASED ALONG THE LOWER NILE, MANY SPECIES OF WILDLIFE HAVE RETREATED UPRIVER.

THE FIRST SETTLERS ALONG the Egyptian Nile shared it with animals such as gazelle, antelopes, wild oxen, jackals, hyenas, leopards and crocodiles. There are none of these animals left today. They were driven away by hunting or by the takeover of their habitats for human settlement. But in the remote gorges of the Blue Nile, and on the White Nile between Victoria Nyanza and Lake Albert, the Nile's large animals survive. Hippos and crocodiles bask in the shallows. Green monkeys, baboons, elephants, buffaloes, impala and waterbucks share the river banks. Although poachers sometimes raid these herds for their skins or their meat, the creation of national parks in Uganda and more recently in Ethiopia ensures greater protection for upriver species.

BIRD LIFE

Human settlement has had less effect on the bird life of the Nile. The lower valley is still a corridor each autumn for migrating birds from south-eastern Europe and Asia heading for winter homes on the upper Nile. These include birds of prey, ducks, waders and swallows. They join some spectacular species which live there permanently. On the lakes of Uganda and Ethiopia there are huge flocks of pink flamingoes, which feed on algae, water insects and shrimps. Fish-eaters include

▼ *A young Nile crocodile basks on the river bank. A fully-grown Nile crocodile can measure up to six metres and weigh over one tonne.*

brightly coloured African kingfishers, one species of which measures up to 46 centimetres, and the sacred ibis, once worshipped in Ancient Egypt but no longer found along the lower Nile.

LIFE IN THE WATER

The building of the Aswan High Dam has brought great changes to the fish life of the lower Nile. Cutting the amount of sediment held in the water has robbed many species of their food, and the pollution of the river by chemical fertilisers has also damaged fish stocks. This has led to an increase in the numbers of more hardy and aggressive fish, such as the Nile perch and the catfish. The loss of sediment food has even had an effect off the coast of the delta, where the once prosperous sardine fishermen are facing smaller catches.

One of the strangest Nile fish is the lungfish, which lives in the swamps and ponds of the White Nile and its tributaries. Unlike most fish, the lungfish can adapt itself to the dry season. When its habitat dries out, it buries

▲ *An African fish-eagle with its prey. Fish-eagles like to hunt mid-morning when the sun is well up and fish rise to the surface. They swoop in low and scoop up the fish in their talons.*

itself in the mud and grows a protective cocoon. It stays in this state of hibernation until the rains come again, when water dissolves the cocoon and releases the fish. If no rain falls, it can stay in deep hibernation, but alive, for up to four years.

THE LESSER FLAMINGO
The lakes of the African Rift Valley are the home of the lesser flamingo, which is over 80 centimetres tall. The flamingoes gather on the lakes in large flocks, feeding on algae floating on or near the surface of the water. If disturbed, the whole flock takes off together, honking like geese, and circles the area until it thinks that it is safe to land again.

◀ *The lungfish has a type of lung that allows it to take in air when there is no water to supply oxygen through its gills.*

TOURISTS ON THE NILE

PROVIDING SERVICES FOR TOURISTS — HOTELS, TRANSPORT AND PLACES TO VISIT — IS AN IMPORTANT INDUSTRY ALONG THE NILE. TOURISTS BRING IN FOREIGN MONEY, WHICH CAN BE USED TO BUY GOODS FROM ABROAD.

TOURISM IS EGYPT'S SECOND most important industry after farming. People visit Egypt mainly to see the monuments of the Ancient Egyptian civilisation at the head of the Nile delta and up the lower valley as far as Aswan.

NILE CRUISES

Many people travel up the valley by luxury cruiser, while others prefer shorter river journeys aboard a felucca, the traditional Egyptian sailing-boat.

The building of the Aswan High Dam has benefited Egypt's tourist trade. Before this, the annual flood restricted the cruising season, but it is now an all-the-year-round business. Cruises on Lake Nasser stop at the re-sited temple at Abu Simbel and other monuments. As Lake Nasser was cut off from the lower Nile by the dam, cruise ships are built at a shipyard on the lakeside.

With a restricted number of places to be visited, all within a narrow valley, there is often great pressure on tourist services. Cruise

▼ *Old and new ways of sailing on the Nile. The sailing-boats are feluccas, traditional Egyptian craft. On the left is a luxury cruiser, the Sun Boat, equipped with restaurants, a sun-deck and comfortable cabins.*

▲*The Blue Nile Gorge, which Ethiopia has begun to develop as one of its tourist attractions.*

ships sometimes have to wait in line at tourist sites or re-arrange their voyages to avoid crowds. Egypt is trying to solve this problem by attracting visitors away from the Nile valley to other places and by appealing to holidaymakers with other interests. Tourist services are being developed in the mountains overlooking the Red Sea, and on the Red Sea itself a beach resort has been built at Hurghada.

MAIN TOURIST SITES IN EGYPT

Giza, on the outskirts of Cairo. Three Great Pyramids, including the **Great Pyramid of Cheops. The Great Sphinx** is nearby.

The Egyptian Museum, Cairo. Over 100,000 objects from Ancient Egypt on display.

Thebes and **Karnak**. Ancient Egyptian temples.

The Valley of the Kings and **The Valley of the Queens**, near Thebes. The latter contains Queen Hatshepsut's temple. Over 130 royal tombs.

Elephantine Island, near Aswan. Ruins of an ancient city, Philae, built in about 2800 BC.

Abu Simbel, above Lake Nasser. The temples and statues of King Rameses II and Queen Nefertari.

▶ *Adventure holidays in the national parks of Uganda and Ethiopia are appealing to increasing numbers of tourists.*

WILDLIFE HOLIDAYS

For many years, Uganda has attracted tourists to its national parks to the north and west of Victoria Nyanza. This kind of holiday used to be for people who were prepared to travel adventurously but uncomfortably. Modern hotels, improved roads and better facilities in the national parks have made it attractive to larger numbers of people, including the all-important family trade.

More recently, Ethiopia has begun to attract tourists, after twenty years in which civil war and drought made it a dangerous country to visit. Since 1991, the government has opened eight national parks and three nature reserves and encouraged local and international companies to build hotels in the most popular tourist spots such as Lake Tana, the Tisisat Falls and the Blue Nile Gorge.

Encouraging tourists to remote regions like these is especially important because it offers local people an extra source of income.

Although tourism is seasonal in areas with a rainy season, providing services for tourists can often be combined with work on the family farm. Tourists also provide a market for local produce and crafts.

THE FUTURE OF THE NILE

ABOUT 150 MILLION PEOPLE — OVER ONE-THIRD OF THEM IN
EGYPT — DEPEND FOR THEIR FUTURE ON THE NILE.

EVEN IN EGYPT the most industrialised of the Nile countries, 45 per cent of the population work on the land. Despite this, Egypt needs to buy 60 per cent of its food from abroad. The population is increasing by about 750, 000 each year. Today, the population of Cairo is nearing 20 million, and by 2050 Egypt's population could number up to 160 million.

THE NEW VALLEY PROJECT

Although it is such a large country, 96 per cent of Egypt is desert. There is a desperate shortage of farming land and living space. One answer is to irrigate more land from the Nile. In 1997 work began on the New Valley Project. The plan, set to be completed in 2020, is to cut a canal 250 kilometres into the desert north-west of Lake Nasser. This will irrigate 2000 square kilometres of desert.

UNDERGROUND WATER

Another possible source of water for Egypt is a huge underground aquifer, or water store. This stretches across North Africa from Egypt

▲ *The unfinished Jonglei Canal in southern Sudan. But if it were to be completed, what effect would it have on Egypt's water supplies?*

▶ *President Mubarak of Egypt gives the signal for work to start on the New Valley Project, launched in 1997. It is expected to take 25 years to complete.*

and Sudan into Libya, and is about 30 metres beneath the desert. Since 1984, Libya has been pumping water out of the aquifer for its own use. So far, Egypt has dug only small wells to reach the water. But each country complains that the other is threatening its own supplies. Exploiting the aquifer fully will depend on international agreement.

CIVIL WAR

In both Sudan and Ethiopia, twenty years of civil war since the 1970s have held back development. In the long years of drought in the 1980s, one million people died of starvation in each country, and another million Ethiopians took refuge from the civil war in neighbouring countries. In the future, both countries are planning to develop their use of the Nile by building dams and

irrigating more land. But this depends on borrowing money abroad. Foreign countries are not keen to lend money to countries with unstable recent histories, especially if this could lead to trouble with Egypt.

CO-OPERATION

Rivers like the Nile, which cross so many national boundaries, need an international body to organise co-operation. The United Nations has suggested setting up a Nile River Commission, representing all the Nile countries, which would carry out this task. There is a good example not far away in southern Africa. The Zambesi river is shared by eight countries, which since 1986 have been working together on a plan for co-operation in using its resources.

▼ *New road schemes cannot keep pace with Cairo's growing traffic. The Egyptian government is trying to ease the problem by building new cities in the desert.*

▲*Development must take into account the needs of all lifestyles, including those in the most remote parts. This Ugandan woman needs the Nile to wash her clothes in.*

GLOSSARY

African Rift Valley a valley formed in north-east Africa by the sinking of the Earth's crust between two fault lines

aquifer a layer of soft rock containing water; this can be pumped off by building wells

barrage a dam built across a river with sluices so that the flow of water can be controlled

camel-train a line of camels, connected by ropes, used by travellers to carry people and goods across the desert

cash crop a crop that the farmer grows to sell

cataract a waterfall or series of rapids

civil war war between people who live in the same country

current (river) the force with which river water flows at a certain point

delta the area of flat land, made up of silt, at the mouth of a river

desertification the spread of the desert to land that was previously grassland

evaporate change from liquid (water) to gas (air) by the action of heat

false-colour satellite image a photograph taken from space that uses unnatural colours to highlight certain features

fault lines cracks in the Earth's crust

felucca a light, narrow boat with one sail

generators machines that convert steam or water power into electricity

gourds the skins of large pumpkins or similar fruit that are dried and used as containers for water

hydro-electric power energy produced by converting the energy of falling water into electricity

ibis a black and white wading bird that feeds on fish

impala a member of the antelope family famous for its ability to leap over obstacles up to three metres high and nine metres long

irrigation canal a canal that carries water from a river to water crops in the fields

minaret the tower of a Muslim mosque from which Muslims are called to prayer

mineral salts chemicals from rocks; they are dissolved in water and are left behind when the water evaporates

mouth (of river) the place where a river meets the sea

nomads people who move from place to place to find food for themselves and their animals

overgrazed (land) land used for food by too many animals so that the grass has no time to grow again

petrochemical industry the manufacture of chemicals from oil

plateau a level area of high land

rapids parts of a river where the water flows fast over rocks

reservoir a natural or artificial lake used for storing water

rising (river) coming out of the ground

sediment ground-down pieces of rock and other material carried along by a river and later deposited on the river banks and bed

silt mud and sand deposited at the mouth of a river

sluice a kind of gate that controls the amount of water allowed to pass through

soil erosion the removal of soil by the action of wind or water

source the starting-point of a river

torrents rushing streams of water

tributaries smaller rivers that flow into a larger river

wash (from ships) the waves that spread from a ship as it passes through the water

waterbuck a kind of antelope that lives in swampy areas

INDEX